POEMS
by
JOANNA
PARKINSON-
HARDMAN
and
Some Celebrity Friends

BBC BOOKS

Published by BBC Books
a division of BBC Enterprises Ltd
Woodlands, 80 Wood Lane, London W12 0TT

First published 1992

ISBN 0 563 36798 9

Typeset by Ace Filmsetting Ltd, Frome, Somerset
Printed in Scotland by Cambus Litho, East Kilbride
and bound by Charles Letts, Dalkeith
Cover printed by Clays Ltd, St Ives plc
Colour separations by Dot Gradations, Essex

From The Honourable Sir Angus Ogilvy, KCVO

Sadly, as many as one in three people in this country still get cancer – but as a result of recent research many more survive. Our scientists now believe that it is no longer a question of 'if' the fight against cancer can be won – but 'when'? The very considerable progress that has been made in recent years is entirely due to the immensely generous help and support that the Imperial Cancer Research Fund has received from literally thousands of people throughout the United Kingdom.

Raising money to finance the necessary research requires very special qualities. It is surprising to find these qualities in one as young as Jo Parkinson-Hardman – who is in fact only ten years old. She is a truly remarkable girl. Many would not be alive today were it not for the enthusiasm, the devotion and the unselfishness of people like Jo.

As President of the Imperial Cancer Research Fund I was delighted when I was told that Esther Rantzen had decided to give her the much coveted *Heart of Gold* Award. I only hope that the magnificent example which she has set will encourage and inspire others to do likewise.

Angus Ogilvy

President ✕ **Imperial Cancer** Research Fund

FOREWORD

The author of this book was ten years old when she was inspired to write her poems, and sell them in aid of the Imperial Cancer Research Fund. She had already raised more than eight hundred pounds through her own efforts, selling her own toys and games, inspiring her friends, family and neighbours to help her fundraise, writing a school magazine, and achieving twelve hours of sponsored silence – no mean achievement when you are ten years old.

The reason Joanna worked so hard to fundraise for cancer research was that her own mother was diagnosed with breast cancer when Joanna was five years old. Another child might have been broken by such tragic news, but Joanna is a fighter, and determined to try and help her mother and all the other cancer sufferers. Her story inspired the other distinguished writers and celebrities whose poems have joined Joanna's in this book, and BBC Books worked their own miracle to rush it into print in time for the special BBC TV *Hearts of Gold* programme in which Joanna herself was honoured.

We must thank all the contributors and everyone who donated time and talent to creating this book. We hope you enjoy it, in the knowledge that in buying it you have also contributed to vital cancer research. And above all we want to congratulate Joanna for having faced tragedy with such outstanding courage, and inspired this book.

Esther Rantzen

Mummy

To my lovely mummy
On Mothers Day,
Whose eyes glisten with love,
May your special day,
Be as peaceful as a dove.

Age 5

Bubbles

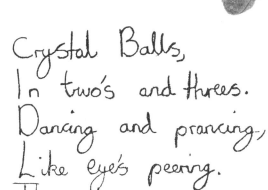

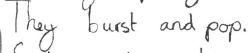

Crystal Balls,
In two's and threes.
Dancing and prancing,
Like eye's peering.
They burst and pop.
Spheres floating high,
Like glittering silver balls.
Flocks of spectrums,
Against the blue sky

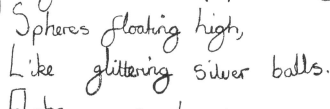

Age 7

Fire works

A brilliant flash of glittering light,
And then BANG it's out of sight.
A glare of colours in the sky,
And then BANG they die.
A puff of smoke and up they go,
And then BANG the colours glow.
They flash, Glow, Glisten and Gleam,
From the roof tops they can be seen.

Age 9

Sounds At Night

Dogs whining,
Cats sighting,
Fountains splashing,
People shouting,
I am trying to get to sleep.
Cars roaring,
Doors banging,
Music booming
I am trying to get to sleep.
Dishes clattering,
Phones ringing,
Will I ever get to sleep.
My eyes are closing,
My clock is ticking away,
I pull the covers over my head,
Hang on a minute,
My mum's calling me,
I must have gone to sleep.
Age 8

Tick Tick Tick Tick Tick Tick Tick Tick

Nature

Nature is a busy thing,
Animals rushing and scurrying about,
You can see them all if you go out.

Age 6

Squirrel

fish

cat

Dog

hedgehogs

Leaves

Leaves, leaves everywhere.
Leaves on trees,
Leaves high,
In the sky,
Leaves down,
On the ground.
Leaves are yellow,
Leaves are brown,
Leaves that float down to the ground.
Leaves, leaves everywhere,
Leaves that float off somewhere.
Leaves that are big,
Leaves that are small
Leaves that float and leaves that fall.
Leaves, leaves everywhere,
Leaves here,
And leaves there.

Age 9

15

The Marvellous New Medicine

The result was rather spectacular,
His legs got fatter and fatter.
His face blew up like a balloon,
I thought he would burst soon.
But he carried on growing,
And puffing and blowing,
Almost reaching the moon.
Just then his mum came out,
She gave a cry, a shriek,
And a terrifying shout.
I didn't know what to do,
To take to my heels,
Or to tell her the truth.
But she soon calmed down,
And gave me a frown,
And wanted an explanation.
Meanwhile in the sky.
He was way up high causing a complication.
Many stood gazing,
With their eyes blazing,
At the giant waving,
While others running, Sheltering under covers,
To get away from the beast.

AAAArrghh

THOMAS

Space Wierd Space

I walked into the space ship,
And Zoomed off into space,
Looking down at my mothers little lost face.
Then it went dark, I quivered with fear,
As outer space began to draw near.
I shot right past the twinkling stars,
To see the planet that they call Mars.
There I discovered aliens in pairs,
Climbing up what seemed like hundreds of stairs.
Suddenly there was a great flash of light,
It was a warning from a satellite,
I went racing to the space shuttle,
When I fell over a spacey puddle.
My ship had been hit by a great meteorite,
I would not be returning home that night.

 Age 8

19

Sandy

When Sandy was 1 he barked on and on.
When Sandy was 2 he chewed up your shoe.
When Sandy was 3 he would sit on your knee.
When Sandy was 4 he would lie by the door.
When Sandy was 5 he would sit on the drive.
When Sandy was 6 he would chase after sticks
When Sandy was 7 he could have walked to Devon
When Sandy was 8 he would sit at the gate.
When Sandy was 9 he felt grand and fine
When Sandy was 10 he was growing slow then
When Sandy was 11 he went to Heaven.

Oh Sandy we all miss you so,
But we understand you had to go.
You have gone into Gods arms,
And out of pain,
So now we know you are happy again.
God bless you Sandy

Age 10

21

The wind

The wind rocks,
The wind sways,
The wind blows in different ways.
Out of all the days,
There is lots of different ways
To show LOVE.

Age 5

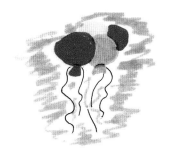

The Practical Joker

She hides behind corners,
And gives you a fright.
She jumps out on you,
 In the middle of the night
So watch out
Be careful
Keep a sharp eye
Just in case she passes you by.

Age 7

California

The golden sands, the lovely beach,
California is the destiny to reach.
The bright blue sea, the surgers on the waves
So join in everyone
We've only got a few days

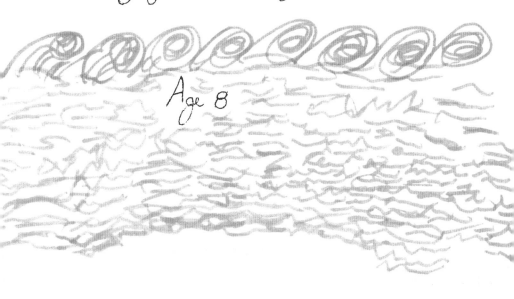

Age 8

Sonnet to a New Love

We fell in love the moment we first met,
You smiled, I smiled, your heart and mine were one.
You had a drink, I tucked you into bed,
You slept and snuggled in the morning sun.
I dreamed about our life together, planned
The glittering treats and treasure we would share,
Your every sob and sigh were my command,
I bought you lace and satin clothes to wear.
And in return you'll take my hand and run,
You'll tease me for a story or a song,
Persuade me throwing mud pies could be fun,
And make me feel so happy, proud and strong.
Some say you should be sweeter, softer, shorter,
I say you're perfect, brand new baby daughter.

Esther Rantzen

When summer comes it's time for cricket,
I like batting and keeping wicket,
But when I bowl I have no luck —
My style is like a ruptured duck.

Gary Lineker

A rolling sea, a lonely gull
Salt spray with kisses stinging
A tumbling wave to soothe the heart
With repose and joy it's bringing

Pauline Collins

If Only Once Again
My Hair Would Sprout

If only once again my hair would sprout,
If what came up matched what was falling out,
To rub the Silvikrin,
On something more than skin,
If only once again my hair would sprout.

In days of yore I grew a healthy crop,
Great tufts of ginger hair stuck out the top,
Luxuriant and plush
Like a lavatory brush
With energy I thought would never stop.

Back then I was extravagantly maned,
I walked about like Hercules unchained,
It was like the burning bush,
Folk said 'Cop the barnet, mush!'
But nowadays me follicles have waned.

Here! Where vigour pulsed down every strand,
Where pretty girls would die to stick their hand,
And barbers were in tears
In the search to find me ears
In the biggest crowning glory in the land.

Imagine! When it started falling out,
I clutched where it had been and there was nowt!
I've lost me prize possession,
One more victim of recession,
Oh if only once again my hair would sprout!

Pam Ayres

A Prayer

One thing I know, life can never die,
Translucent, splendid, flaming like the sun.
Only our bodies wither and deny
The Life Force when our strength is done.

We all transmit this wonderful fire,
Its force and power from God above
And know eternally it is His
In every act of love.

Dame Barbara Cartland, D.B.E., D.St.J.

It's Lovely Here

I like it here, on blasted rocks
a heat haze on the sea
and salt water over me.
I like the changes
one moment dry and baked
the next – exhilaration fresh and pure.

I like it here, I like the space
there's room to think
and life to drink.
Seagulls artful over head
summer noises from a distant beach
breathe deep . . .
and taste the cascading fragrance of coconut oil.

I love it here, my dreaming place
an endless ocean heaving
leaving me believing
there's so much more
than drying seaweed
and forgotten low tide fishing line.

I'm happy here, don't get me wrong
it's not the tranquillity
just the immobility.
Out there experience beyond belief
the enormity of all there is.
Where does a young limpet begin?

Phillip Schofield

I like chocolate
Yum Yum Yum
Maybe that's why
I've got a big tum . . .

Dawn French

Life

I have four dogs but only
two hands for stroking –
that's what life's about:

– racing from dog to
dog to hug them
– so nobody's left out.

Jilly Cooper

The Magic Pebble

My favourite thing is a pebble
That I found on a beach in Wales
It looks like any other
But its magic never fails

It does my homework for me
Makes difficult sums seem clear
School dinners taste delicious
It makes teachers disappear

It turns water into lemonade
A bully into a frog
When I'm in need of company
It becomes a friendly dog

Close your eyes, make a wish
And you're in a foreign land
Space travel is so easy
Simply hold it in your hand

My favourite thing is a pebble
Its magic, honestly.
I couldn't bear to be without it
(. . . But its yours for 20p)

Roger McGough

The Things I Like Best

The things I like best, the things that are ace,
Are my frequent journeys into OUTERSPACE.
All I have to do, if I have the time,
Is get on my bed, that is: get supine.
It's a lovely feeling as I gaze at the ceiling;
My thoughts floating free in that far Galaxy.
I then close my eyes and I start to rise,
Up through the roof and over the town;
Up through the clouds and when I look down,
The Earth is a ball that turns to a dot.
My worries and troubles are all forgot!
I'm happy and drifting and what's that I hear?
A voice that's familiar and incredibly clear!
'What's that in the oven? It's all gooey and black!'
It's the bloody dinner, I'd better get back!

Julie Walters

One of my favourite things to me
Is sitting in bed on Sunday
with a cup of tea
My remote control at the ready
All set to watch my favourite
programme on the TV
Which is *Little House on the Prairie*
(By the way – poetry never was my fortee!)

Michaela Strachan

Favourites

jack-in-the-boxes without springs
jackdaws without wings
lumberjacks with broken backs
and both their arms in slings
these are a few of my favourite images

John Hegley

My favourite things are somewhat eclectic,
Like giggling lifeguards and cows apoplectic,
Luminous bin liners, burglars called Joyce,
Quite a remarkably catholic choice.

Girls with verruccas and men with hot flushes,
Snowflakes with gravy and gossiping thrushes,
Silver tomatoes and leeks transcendental,
Cream cakes with anchovies, some ornamental.

Graphic graffiti and sugar free poodles,
Concrete marshmallows and Fergie's old doodles,
Adjustable elbows, a hanky that sings,
Aren't they mundane, all my favourite things?

Maureen Lipman

My Favourite Thing

My favourite thing is my teddy bear,
He's 48 and he's got no hair,
My Nanny bought him after the war
and gave him to me as I sat on the floor.
Around his neck is a white and blue scarf,
And whenever I see him he still makes me laugh.
He was cuddled so much that he lost his head,
So I sewed it back on with some purperly thread.
My dog chewed his tummy in '86
Which left him in a bit of a fix.
But I soon made a new one of yellowy cotton
And now he doesn't feel nearly so rotten.
No gold nor silver nor diamond ring
Can compare with my Teddy. My favourite thing!

Lynn Redgrave

My Favourite Things

Crystal-clear, warmth, gold,
Lapping sea, horizon, peace.
Laughter, giggles, pranks,
Friends, days, weeks.

Words, clever, picture,
Imagine, travel, time.
Favourite things, words,
in my mind rhyme

Mike Smith

The sea is now so calm and blue,
Though sailing boats are moving through
The ripples shimmering in the sun
And children on the beach have fun.
But watch how quickly this can alter.
Dark clouds scattering make us falter
Into a mad tempestuous scene,
As the stormy clouds above us lean,
Waves suddenly pound the shore.
No one can step within it now, or
Would too soon be swept away.
Thankfully fun will be had another day.

Gloria Hunniford

I'd really like to do a poem,
but my brain don't seem to grow 'em.
It is, therefore, not a case of shan't
but more a case of simply can't!

Paul Daniels

Thank You

Thank you for the world so sweet;
Thank you for the food we eat;
Thank you for the birds that sing:
Thank you, God, for everything!
E. RUTTER LEATHAM

Thank you for my favourite hymns;
Thank you for my healthy limbs;
Thank you for the Suffolk coast;
Thank you, God, for cheese on toast.

Thanks for making flowers grow;
Thank you for the radio;
Thank you for the stars that shine;
Thank you, God, for sparkling wine.

Thanks for grass and thanks for trees;
Thanks for public libraries;
Thank you for my own front door;
Thank you, God, for *LA Law*.

Thank you for my new guitar;
Thank you for my little car;
Thank you for reposeful nights;
Thank you, God, for Lycra tights.

Thank you for the swimming-pool,
And for all I learned at school;
Thank you for the string quartet;
Thank you, God, for Nicorette.

Thank you for this day so glad;
Thank you for 'A Shropshire Lad';
Thanks for Mozart, thanks for Bach;
Thank you, God, for Dulwich Park.

Thank you for the world so sweet;
Thank you for the food we eat;
Thank you for the birds that sing:
Thank you, God, for everything!

Wendy Cope

ACKNOWLEDGEMENTS

BBC Books would like to thank the following companies who have given generously of their time and resources towards the production of this book:

Ace Filmsetting Ltd, Frome, Somerset
Cambus Litho Ltd, East Kilbride, Scotland
Clays Ltd, St Ives plc
Dot Gradations, Woodham Ferrers, Essex
The Graphic Unit, London N1
Charles Letts, Dalkeith, Scotland
Superchrome Services Ltd, London NW1

They would also like to thank Camera Press for the use of the photograph of Sir Angus Ogilvy by Snowdon.